OLYMPIC HEROES AND ZEROS

Robin Johnson

Crabtree Publishing Company
www.crabtreebooks.com

Crabtree Publishing Company

www.crabtreebooks.com

Author: Robin Johnson
Publishing plan research and development:
 Sean Charlebois, Reagan Miller
 Crabtree Publishing Company
Photo research: Robin Johnson, Rachel Minay
Editors: Rachel Minay, Kathy Middleton
Design: Tim Mayer (Mayer Media)
Cover design: Margaret Amy Salter
Production and print coordinator:
 Katherine Berti
Prepress technician: Katherine Berti

Produced for Crabtree Publishing by
White-Thomson Publishing

Reading levels determined by
Publishing Solutions Group.
Content level: P
Readability level: L

Photographs:
Corbis: Bettmann: pp. 20, 23, 30, 36–37;
Duomo: p. 10; Filippo Monteforte/epa: p.
19; JOHN G.MABANGLO/epa: pp. 40–41;
PCN: pp. 42–43; Reuters: pp. 32–33; Tang
Shi/xh/Xinhua Press: pp. 16–17; Wang
Yuguo/xh/Xinhua Press: pp. 34–35;
Dreamstime: Asterixvs: p. 26; Fletch1959:
pp. 4–5; Graphitec: p. 27; Marclschauer: p.
45; Wickedgood: p. 28; Getty Images:
pp.12–13, 31, pp. 38–39; AFP: pp. 6–7, 22,
44–45; Popperfoto: pp. 8–9, 18–19; Sports
Illustrated: pp. 14–15, 24–25; Shutterstock:
front and back cover; catwalker: pp. 3, 21;
Neftali: p. 29; Ververidis Vasilis: pp. 1, 10–
11; Thinkstock: front cover.

Library and Archives Canada Cataloguing in Publication

Johnson, Robin (Robin R.)
 Olympic heroes and zeros / Robin Johnson.

(Crabtree chrome)
Includes index.
Issued also in electronic formats.
ISBN 978-0-7787-7930-8 (bound).--ISBN 978-0-7787-7939-1
(pbk.)

 1. Olympic athletes--Biography--Juvenile literature.
2. Olympics--History--Juvenile literature. I. Title. II. Series:
Crabtree chrome

GV697.A1J64 2012   j796.48092'2   C2012-907047-5

Library of Congress Cataloging-in-Publication Data

CIP available at Library of Congress

Crabtree Publishing Company

Printed in the U.S.A./112012/FA20121012

www.crabtreebooks.com   1-800-387-7650

Published in Canada
Crabtree Publishing
616 Welland Ave.
St. Catharines, ON
L2M 5V6

Published in the United States
Crabtree Publishing
PMB 59051
350 Fifth Avenue, 59th Floor
New York, New York 10118

Published in the United Kingdom
Crabtree Publishing
Maritime House
Basin Road North, Hove
BN41 1WR

Published in Australia
Crabtree Publishing
3 Charles Street
Coburg North
VIC 3058

Contents

Record Breakers

Faster, Higher, Stronger

The Summer Olympics are an international sports event held every four years. The world's best athletes come together to compete for their countries. The athletes all try to run, ride, swim, shoot, paddle, fight, jump, and throw their way to **glory**.

▲ *New heroes and zeros were made at the 2012 Olympics in London.*

Heroes and Zeros

Most athletes find the strength and courage to succeed on their own. These athletes become Olympic heroes. But some athletes crack under the pressure of Olympic competition. They lie, cheat, and do whatever it takes to win.

"The most important thing in the Olympic Games is not winning but taking part."

Pierre de Coubertin, founder of the modern Olympic Games

glory: great honor or praise for doing something important.

Medal Machine

Michael Phelps is a medal machine. The U.S. swimmer has won an incredible 22 Olympic medals. He has 18 golds, two silvers, and two bronze medals. The swimming champ has smashed records in both individual and **relay** events.

▲ *Phelps swims to gold in the 100-meter butterfly final at the London Games, 2012.*

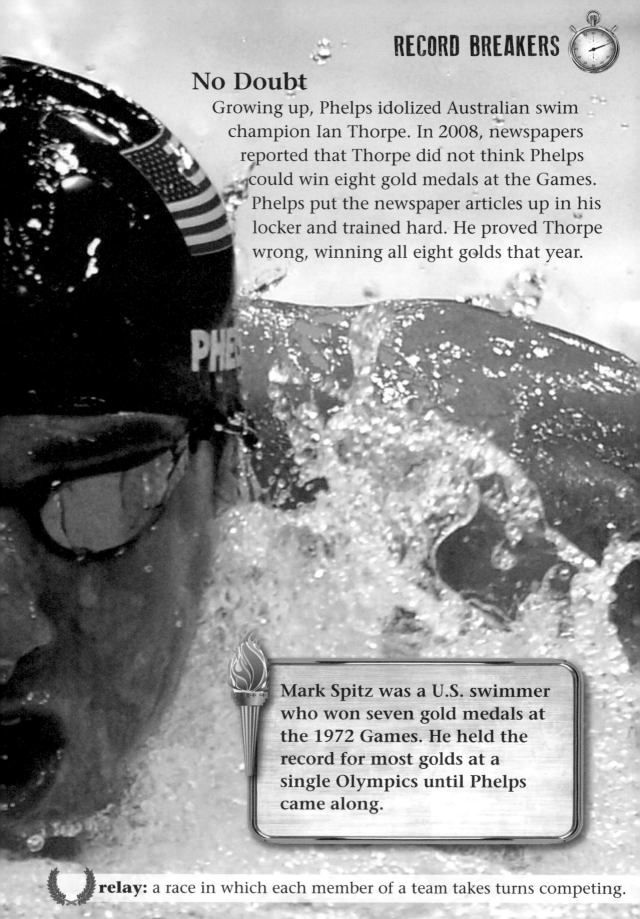

No Doubt

Growing up, Phelps idolized Australian swim champion Ian Thorpe. In 2008, newspapers reported that Thorpe did not think Phelps could win eight gold medals at the Games. Phelps put the newspaper articles up in his locker and trained hard. He proved Thorpe wrong, winning all eight golds that year.

Mark Spitz was a U.S. swimmer who won seven gold medals at the 1972 Games. He held the record for most golds at a single Olympics until Phelps came along.

relay: a race in which each member of a team takes turns competing.

Golden Girl

Larisa Latynina has won more Olympic medals than any other woman. The Russian gymnast won an amazing nine gold medals. She also won five silver medals and four bronze medals from 1956 to 1964.

▶ *Larissa Latynina held the record for most Olympic medals from 1964 to 2012. She still holds the record for the most Olympic medals in individual events.*

Flying Solo

Latynina won a medal every time she took part in an Olympic event—except once. In 1956, she came in fourth place on the balance beam. Incredibly, Latynina held the record for most Olympic medals until 2012! Michael Phelps' victories in London pushed his total of 22 medals past Latynina's total of 18.

U.S. swimmer Trischa Zorn is the golden girl of the Paralympics. The Paralympic Games is an international sports event for athletes with physical or intellectual **impairment**. Zorn—who is blind—has won an astounding 41 gold medals!

impairment: a physical or intellectual limitation.

Lightning Bolt

Jamaican runner Usain Bolt is the fastest man in the world. At the 2008 Games, he ran the 100-meter race in just 9.69 seconds! Four years later, "Lightning Bolt" struck again. He beat his own Olympic record, crossing the finish line in just 9.63 seconds.

◄ *Flo-Jo celebrates a win at the 1988 Olympic Trials.*

▼ *Usain Bolt gives the crowd his famous "lightning bolt" pose.*

Going the Distance

Bolt also bolted down the track in the 200-meter and 4x100-meter **sprints**. He won both events at the 2008 and 2012 Games. Each time he won, the entertaining track star struck his famous lightning bolt pose for the crowd. "I'm now a legend," he said.

Although she died in 1998, U.S. runner Florence Griffith-Joyner (Flo-Jo) still holds the record for the women's 100-meter and 200-meter sprints. She is also remembered for her famous long and colorful fingernails and her one-legged racing suits.

sprints: short running races.

Anything to Win

From Hero...

Canadian sprinter Ben Johnson dashed to glory in the 1988 Games in Seoul, South Korea. He won the 100-meter race with a world-record time of 9.79 seconds. Canadians went wild with joy. Newspapers called Johnson the "King of Seoul."

▶ *Canadian runner Ben Johnson became a hero in less than ten seconds. Carl Lewis (far right) also beat the world record in the same race.*

...to Zero

Three days later, the king lost his crown. People were shocked to find out that "Big Ben" had tested positive for use of **steroids**. Johnson's gold medal and world record were immediately taken away. The Canadian government investigated the scandal. Now Canada is a leader in the fight against steroid use in sports.

The medal was awarded to U.S. runner Carl Lewis. An American track star, Lewis won a total of nine Olympic gold medals in sprints and long jump events.

steroids: illegal drugs that can make athletes stronger and faster.

Marion's Medals

Marion Jones won five medals in track and field at the 2000 Olympics. Seven years later, the U.S. athlete admitted she had used steroids. Jones was forced to return her medals in **shame**. She also served six months in prison for lying in court about her steroid use.

▲ *Neither Marion Jones (leading the pack) nor Katerina Thanou (in second place) ended up with the gold medal.*

No Gold for You!

Most of the medals were given to other athletes. No gold medal was ever awarded for the 100-meter race, though. Judges suspected that silver medalist Katerina Thanou had used steroids, too. The Greek runner faked a motorcycle crash to avoid drug testing!

"It's with a great amount of **shame** that I stand before you ... I have let my country down, and I have let myself down."

Marion Jones

 shame: strong feelings of guilt for doing something wrong.

▲ *Yu Yang (left), one of the disgraced badminton players from China, quit the sport immediately after the Olympics.*

Doubles Trouble

In the recent Olympic Games in London, four women's doubles badminton teams were thrown out for cheating. The teams, who came from China, Indonesia, and South Korea, had not cheated to win their games, however. They had tried to lose!

Lose Your Way to the Top

In the "**round robin**" tournament, winners of one match would move on to meet winners of another match. But the women lost their games on purpose so they could face losing teams instead in upcoming matches. The pairs served into the net and missed easy shots. Fans booed as the world's best players played some terrible badminton.

> "It was absolutely shocking. The crowds were booing and chanting 'Off, off, off.'"
>
> 2004 badminton silver medalist Gail Emms

round robin: an event in which teams play each other in turn.

Driven to Win

In 1904, Fred Lorz sped to the finish line of the marathon—in a car! The U.S. long-distance runner hitched a ride for part of the 25-mile (40-km) race. He later got out and was the first to walk across the finish line!

▼ *Lorz, seen here at the start of the 1904 Olympic marathon, is number 31. Thomas Hicks (number 20) was declared the winner after Lorz was found out.*

Fan Out

Even Olympic fans can be zeros. During the 2004 marathon, a man jumped out of the crowd lining the streets of Athens. He tackled the runner in the lead, Brazil's Vanderlei de Lima. De Lima managed to break free and win the bronze medal, finishing the race with a playful, flying dance. He was also given a special medal for **sportsmanship**.

◄ *De Lima is tackled by a spectator during the 2004 Olympic Games. This moment may have cost him the gold medal.*

"It was very difficult for me to finish. With my sense of Olympic spirit I showed my determination and won a medal."

Vanderlei de Lima

sportsmanship: fairness and good behavior in a competition.

19

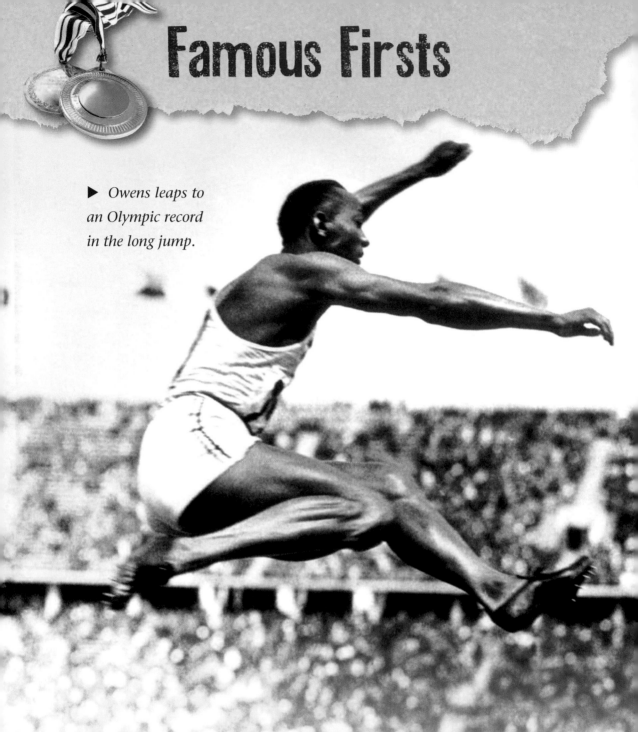

Famous Firsts

▶ *Owens leaps to an Olympic record in the long jump.*

Olympic Owens

In 1936, three years before the start of World War II, the Olympics hit the big screen. German leader Adolf Hitler showed the Berlin Games on large TV screens around the city. Hitler wanted to prove that white Germans were the best athletes in the world. An African-American named Jesse Owens **foiled** Hitler's plan.

▲ *This U.S. postage stamp was made in 1990 to celebrate what Jesse Owens achieved at the 1936 Games.*

On Track

Owens won four gold medals in track and field. He was the first American ever to do so. Owens won the 100-meter and 200-meter sprints, the 4x100-meter relay, and the long jump. He also set three world records. Owens did everything right—and he proved Hitler wrong.

> "The road to the Olympics leads to no city, no country. The road to the Olympics leads ... to the best within us."
>
> Jesse Owens

 foiled: ruined or kept someone from succeeding.

Perfect 10

In 1976, Nadia Comaneci scored a perfect 10 on the uneven bars in Montreal. The young Romanian was the first gymnast ever to perform a **flawless** routine at the Olympics. No one thought a perfect 10.00 was possible. In fact, scoreboards had room for only three numbers. Comaneci's score was shown as 1.00 instead of 10.00!

▶ *Comaneci was just 14 years old in 1976. Today, gymnasts must be at least 16 years old or turn 16 during an Olympic year to compete at the Games.*

Youngest All-Around

Comaneci went on to earn six more perfect scores at the Games that year. She won gold in the bars, balance beam, and individual all-around events. At just 14 years old, Comaneci was the youngest gymnast ever to win the all-around title.

▲ *A perfect performance on the balance beam won Comaneci another gold.*

"Hard work has made it easy. That is my secret. That is why I win."

Nadia Comaneci

flawless: perfect.

Dream Team

In the Barcelona Games in 1992, the U.S. men's basketball team was called the "Dream Team." It was the first time the Olympic team was allowed to have **professional** players from the NBA. It was also the first time that any team had scored over 100 points in each one of their games!

▲ *The Dream Team was one of the strongest teams ever put together in any sport.*

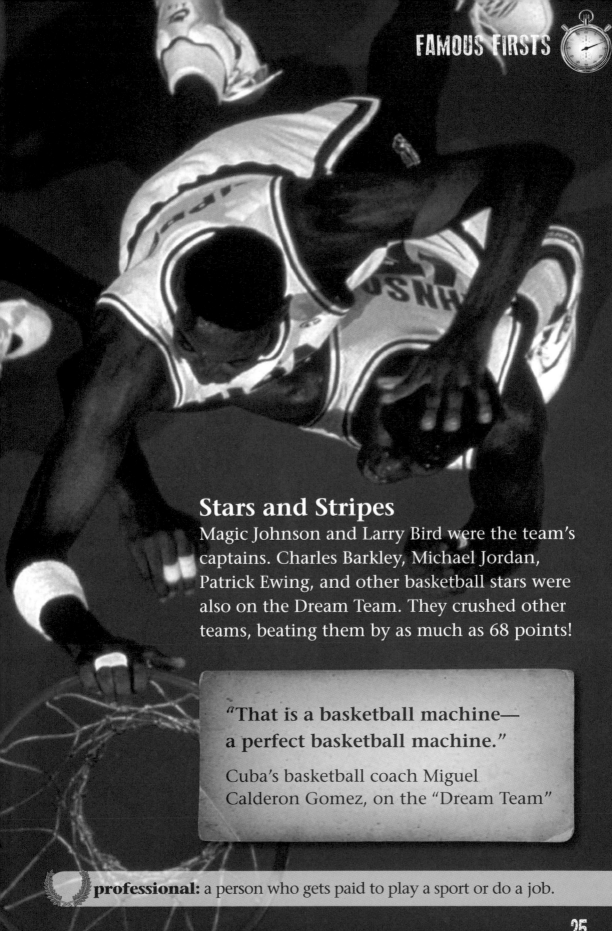

Stars and Stripes

Magic Johnson and Larry Bird were the team's captains. Charles Barkley, Michael Jordan, Patrick Ewing, and other basketball stars were also on the Dream Team. They crushed other teams, beating them by as much as 68 points!

"That is a basketball machine—a perfect basketball machine."

Cuba's basketball coach Miguel Calderon Gomez, on the "Dream Team"

professional: a person who gets paid to play a sport or do a job.

▶ *While he was still at school, Pistorius took part in rugby, tennis, Olympic wrestling and water polo. He started running in 2004—and he hasn't stopped since!*

In the Fast Lane

Oscar Pistorius is called the "fastest man on no legs." Born with a medical condition that cost him both legs below the knee, the South African athlete runs on curved metal blades. Pistorius competed at the 2008 Paralympic Games and won the 100-meter, 200-meter, and 400-meter races. But he wanted to compete in the Olympic Games, too.

Blade Runner

Pistorius argued that his blades did not give him an advantage over other runners. In 2012, he became the first **amputee** allowed to compete in an Olympic race. Pistorius ran in the 400-meter race and came second in his heat (an early round). He also competed in the 2012 Paralympics and won gold medals in the 400-meter race and the 4x100-meter relay.

> "You're not disabled by the disabilities you have, you are able by the abilities you have."
>
> Oscar Pistorius

◀ *Oscar Pistorius is an inspiration to millions of young athletes worldwide.*

amputee: a person whose arm or leg has been removed.

Fighting for Gold

The Greatest

U.S. boxer Cassius Clay knocked out the competition at the 1960 Games in Rome. He easily defeated his **opponents** and became the light heavyweight champ. Clay returned home to the United States a hero. He was still treated like a zero, however.

▼ *Cassius Clay (later Muhammad Ali) called himself "the greatest." He earned his nickname in many boxing matches.*

◀ *Before one boxing match, Ali said that he would "float like a butterfly, sting like a bee."*

Fighting for His Rights

Back home, a waitress refused to serve Clay because he was black. He threw his gold medal into a river in disgust. Clay—who later changed his name to Muhammad Ali—went on to become one of the greatest boxers of all time.

> "Champions are made from something they have deep inside them—a desire, a dream, a vision."
>
> Muhammad Ali

 opponents: people who compete against others.

Winning Gold

The modern pentathlon is an Olympic sport made up of five events—épée fencing, shooting, swimming, horse riding and cross-country running. In 1976, in Montreal, Russian fencer Boris Onishchenko cheated. In épée matches, a fencer earns points when their electronic sword touches an opponent's body. Onishchenko fixed his sword so he could control when it showed a hit.

▲ *Boris Onishchenko cheated so he could get a medal.*
Instead, he got the nickname "Boris the Cheat."

Caught!

Onishchenko was good at fencing but bad at cheating. His sword went off when he was too far from his opponents. Judges took the sword from him to inspect it. Onishchenko won the match using a regular sword. He was later **disqualified** for cheating.

▲ *Jim Fox (on the left in this picture) played Onishchenko in the épée match. This British team went on to win gold in the modern pentathlon.*

> "It was like waving a magic wand."
>
> Fencer Jim Fox, who faced Onishchenko at the 1976 Games

 disqualified: removed from competition for breaking the rules.

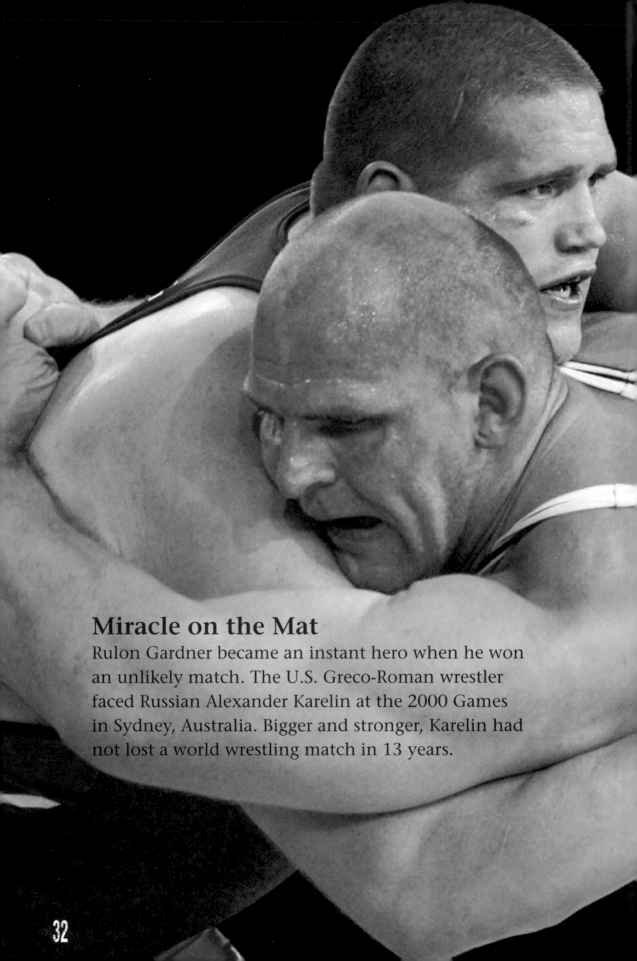

Miracle on the Mat

Rulon Gardner became an instant hero when he won
an unlikely match. The U.S. Greco-Roman wrestler
faced Russian Alexander Karelin at the 2000 Games
in Sydney, Australia. Bigger and stronger, Karelin had
not lost a world wrestling match in 13 years.

Rulon Rules

Gardner had never even come close to winning a world event. No one thought he could beat the mighty Russian champ. However, Gardner believed in himself. He fought hard and beat Karelin 1-0 in a stunning upset for the gold medal.

"It's not a dreaming story. It's not Harry Potter. It's a real-life story ... and what better way to show kids their **potential** than with a real-life story?"

Rulon Gardner

◄ *Gardner (top) holds Karelin in the gold medal match. During the match, Gardner told himself, "I think I can, I think I can."*

potential: the ability to succeed in the future.

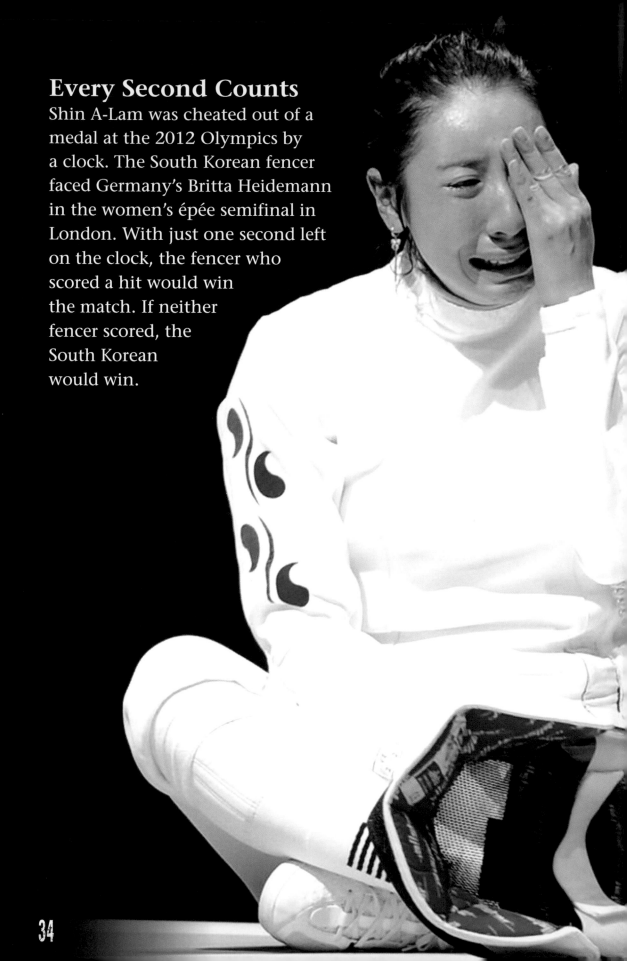

Every Second Counts

Shin A-Lam was cheated out of a medal at the 2012 Olympics by a clock. The South Korean fencer faced Germany's Britta Heidemann in the women's épée semifinal in London. With just one second left on the clock, the fencer who scored a hit would win the match. If neither fencer scored, the South Korean would win.

began fencing, however. After a few seconds, Heidemann made a hit and won the match. The rules would not allow A-Lam to leave the playing area while her team **appealed** the timekeeping error. She sat on the floor for more than an hour before being told she had lost.

Shin A-Lam fought back at the 2012 Games. She went on to win a silver medal in the women's team épée event in London.

◀ *Shin A-Lam had the crowd's sympathy as she sat waiting for the judge's decision.*

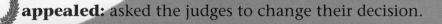

appealed: asked the judges to change their decision.

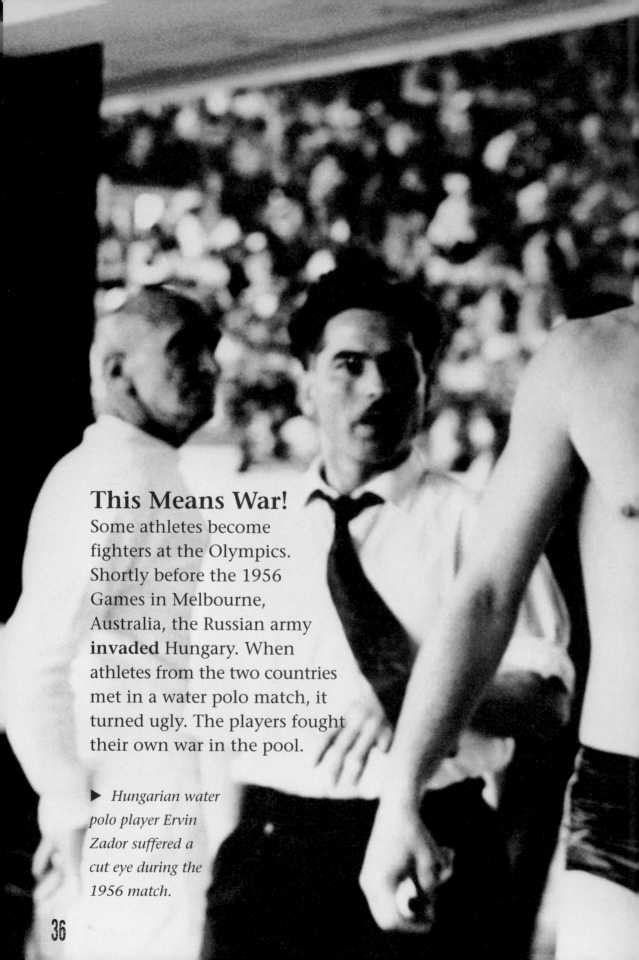

This Means War!

Some athletes become fighters at the Olympics. Shortly before the 1956 Games in Melbourne, Australia, the Russian army **invaded** Hungary. When athletes from the two countries met in a water polo match, it turned ugly. The players fought their own war in the pool.

▶ *Hungarian water polo player Ervin Zador suffered a cut eye during the 1956 match.*

Blood in the Water

The athletes swore and hit and kicked each other. The water turned red from their blood. The Hungarians were knocked down but not out. They won the match and went on to win the gold medal.

The 1956 water polo match was called off early so the angry crowd would not storm the pool.

invaded: entered a place by force to take over or destroy it.

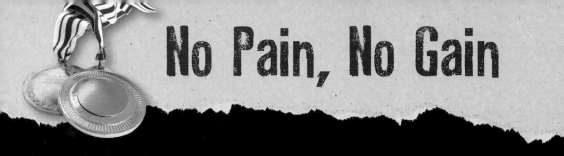

Laumann's Leg

Sometimes athletes get hurt before the Olympics begin.
They battle back and become heroes of the Games.
Canadian rower Silken Laumann had a brutal accident
before the start of the 1992 Olympics. An opponent's
boat rammed into hers and smashed her leg to pieces.

▼ *Silken Laumann pushed
through the pain as she pulled
her boat through the water.*

Battling Back

Laumann had been a favorite to win a gold medal in the Barcelona Games, but doctors said she might never row again. She had five operations and spent three weeks in the hospital. When Laumann got out, she trained long and hard. Just ten weeks after the accident, Laumann won a bronze medal for Canada!

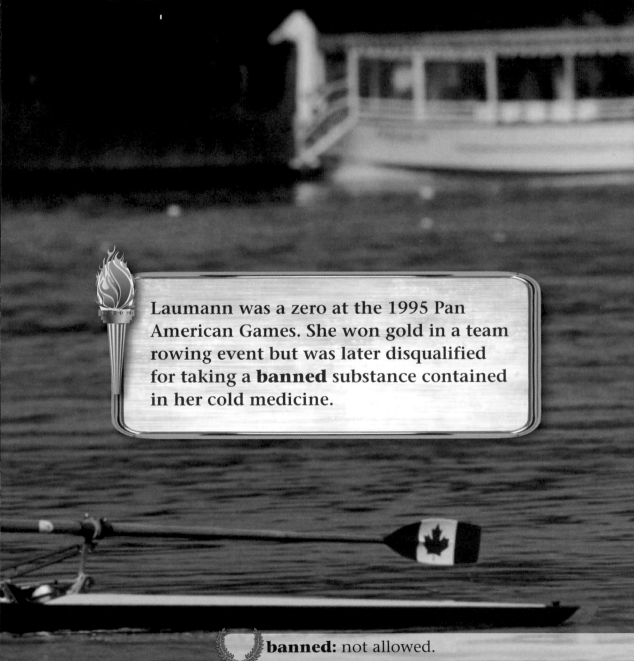

Laumann was a zero at the 1995 Pan American Games. She won gold in a team rowing event but was later disqualified for taking a **banned** substance contained in her cold medicine.

banned: not allowed.

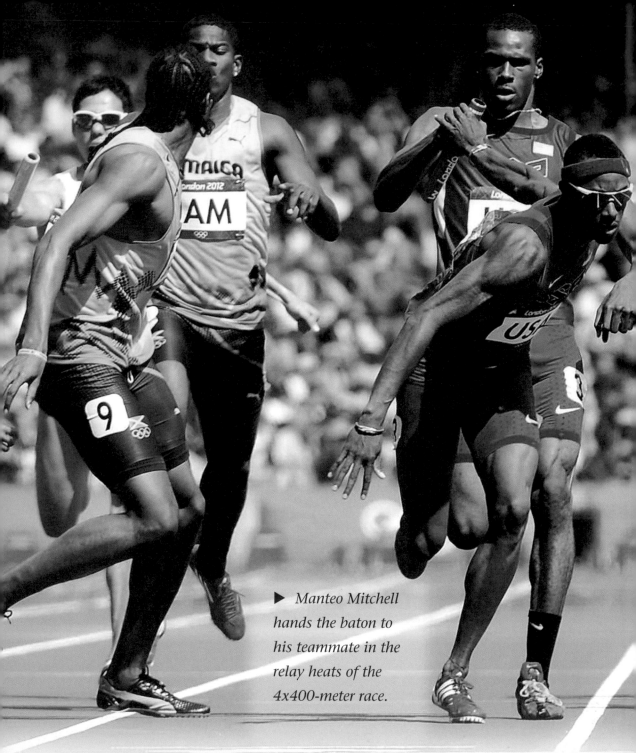

▶ *Manteo Mitchell hands the baton to his teammate in the relay heats of the 4x400-meter race.*

Pushing Through the Pain

Some athletes get hurt during Olympic competition. They push through the pain and become heroes. At the 2012 Games in London, American runner Manteo Mitchell ran the first **leg** of an early 4x400-meter relay race. Mitchell had slipped on stairs a few days before the Games but felt fine.

Break a Leg

Halfway through his part of the race, a bone in his left leg suddenly broke. The runner heard a pop and then felt extreme pain. But Mitchell kept going and finished the race. Incredibly, the American team qualified for the final race. They picked up the silver medal, only this time without Mitchell.

"I heard it and I felt it. But I figured it's what almost any person would've done in that situation."
Manteo Mitchell

 leg: one section of a relay race.

Vaulting to Gold

U.S. gymnast Kerri Strug made the biggest landing of her life at the 1996 Games in Atlanta. Her team needed to win the vault to jump ahead of the Russians for gold. Strug was the last gymnast to compete in the final event.

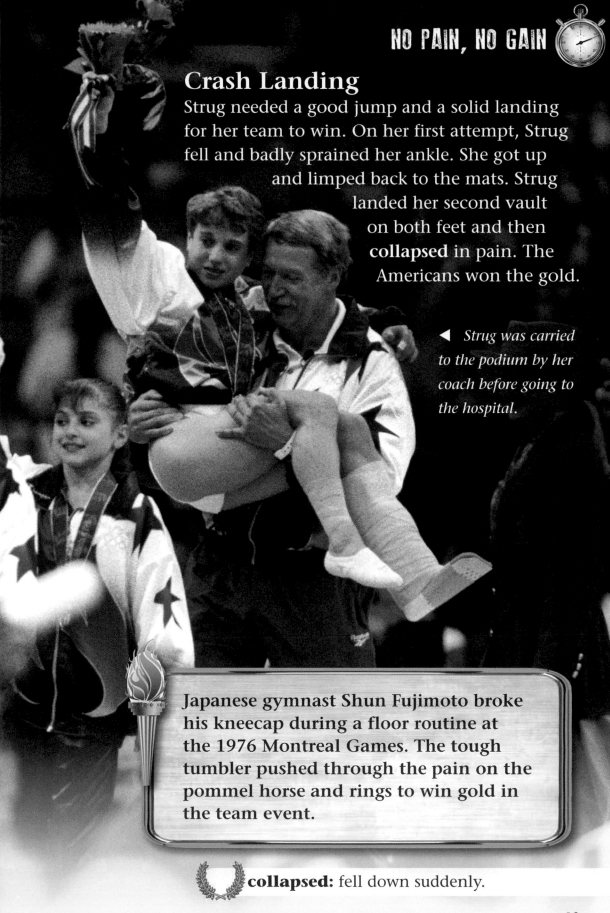

Crash Landing

Strug needed a good jump and a solid landing for her team to win. On her first attempt, Strug fell and badly sprained her ankle. She got up and limped back to the mats. Strug landed her second vault on both feet and then **collapsed** in pain. The Americans won the gold.

◀ *Strug was carried to the podium by her coach before going to the hospital.*

Japanese gymnast Shun Fujimoto broke his kneecap during a floor routine at the 1976 Montreal Games. The tough tumbler pushed through the pain on the pommel horse and rings to win gold in the team event.

collapsed: fell down suddenly.

Big Finish

Sometimes the biggest heroes at the Olympics do not take home medals. At the 1992 Games, it looked as though British runner Derek Redmond would win the 400-meter semifinal race. Then a muscle in his thigh tore.

▲ Derek Redmond made his father—and his country—proud at the 1992 Games.

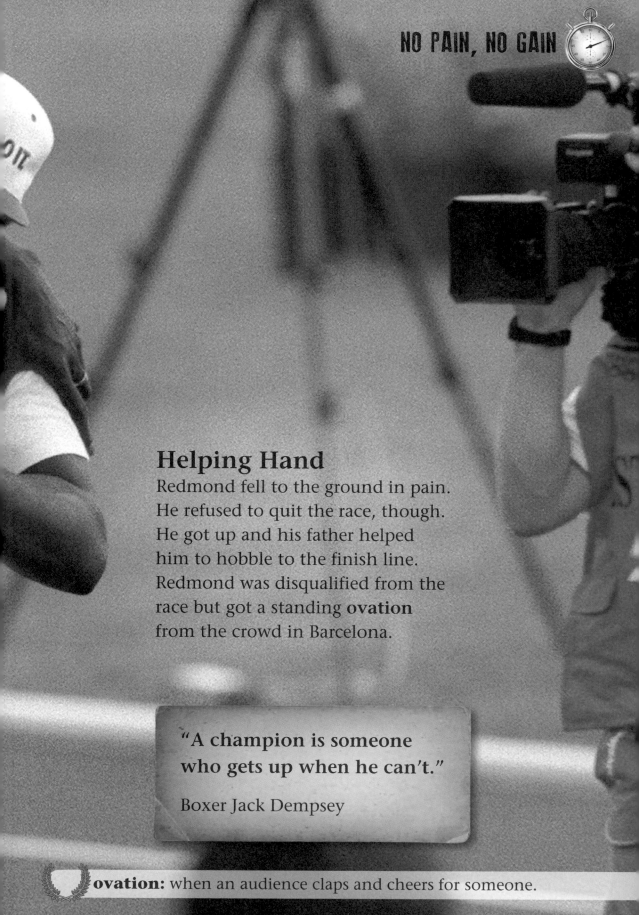

Helping Hand

Redmond fell to the ground in pain.
He refused to quit the race, though.
He got up and his father helped
him to hobble to the finish line.
Redmond was disqualified from the
race but got a standing **ovation**
from the crowd in Barcelona.

"A champion is someone
who gets up when he can't."

Boxer Jack Dempsey

ovation: when an audience claps and cheers for someone.

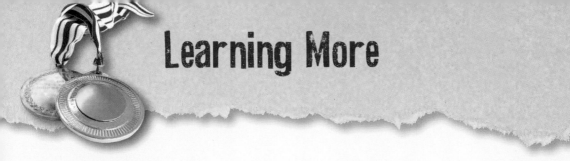

Learning More

Books

Gold Medal for Weird by Kevin Sylvester (Kids Can Press, 2007)

Great Moments in the Summer Olympics by Matt Christopher (Little, Brown Books for Young Readers, 2012)

Swifter, Higher, Stronger: A Photographic History of the Summer Olympics by Sue Macy (National Geographic Society, 2008)

The Olympic Games by Dorling Kindersley (Dorling Kindersley Limited, 2004)

Websites

www.olympic.org
The official website of the Olympics.

www.paralympic.org
The official website of the Paralympics.

Glossary

amputee A person whose arm or leg has been removed

appealed Asked the judges to change their decision

banned Not allowed

collapsed Fell down suddenly

disqualified Removed from competition for breaking the rules

flawless Perfect

foiled Ruined or kept someone from succeeding

glory Great honor or praise for doing something important

impairment A physical or intellectual limitation

invaded Entered a place by force to take over or destroy it

leg One section of a relay race

opponents People who compete against others

ovation When an audience claps and cheers for someone

potential The ability to succeed in the future

professional A person who gets paid to play a sport or do a job

relay A race in which each member of a team takes turns competing

round robin An event in which teams play each other in turn

shame Strong feelings of guilt for doing something wrong

sportsmanship Fairness and good behavior in a competition

sprints Short running races

steroids Illegal drugs that can make athletes stronger and faster

Index

Entries in **bold** refer to pictures